# WHERE'S MY PRESENT?

HODDER
Wayland

an imprint of Hodder Children's Books

# New Experiences

Are We There Yet? My First Holiday
Can I Feed It? My First Pet
I Want That Room! Moving House
I'm Still Important! A New Baby
Open Wide! My First Trip to the Dentist
Say Aah! My First Visit to the Doctor
Where's My Peg? My First Day at School
Where's My Present? My First Party

Published in Great Britain in 2000 by Hodder Wayland,
an imprint of Hodder Children's Books
© Copyright 2000 Hodder Wayland

Editor: Jason Hook
Designer: Tessa Barwick

A Catalogue record for this book is available from the British Library.

ISBN 0 7502 2650 1

Printed and bound in Italy by G. Canale & C.Sp.A., Turin

Hodder Children's Books
A division of Hodder Headline Limited
338 Euston Road, London NW1 3BH

# WHERE'S MY PRESENT?

## My first Party

Written by Jen Green

Illustrated by Mike Gordon

an imprint of Hodder Children's Books

Last week the postman brought
a letter with my name on it.
It was from my friend Josh.

He was having a fancy dress party for his birthday, and he had invited me!

Come to Joshua's party. fancy dress Saturday 18th July 3.00 pm

I had never been to a fancy dress party before. Mum said everyone would have a costume.

'We'll buy a present for Josh,' said Mum. 'And I'll make you a costume.'

Next day we went to the toyshop and bought Josh a kite. I wanted a kite too, but Dad said we were only buying one for Josh.

I put on my costume and Mum painted my face. I was a tiger!

I asked Mum if my birthday was coming soon, but she said it wasn't for a long time yet.

Dad took me to the party.
When we arrived, I felt shy.

Then I saw my friends Kate
and Oliver. Their costumes
were really funny.

Josh had loads of presents.
Did he really need one
from me?

**Wow, thanks!**

Then Josh asked,
'Where's my present?'
So I handed it over.

We played musical statues. When the music stopped, you had to stand very still.

Everyone wobbled except
for Kate, who won a prize.

Then we played pass the parcel.
The music stopped when I had
the parcel.

I unwrapped the paper, but there was more paper underneath!

We had tea next. There were
sandwiches, crisps, cakes,
jelly and ice-cream.
20

I sat next to a girl called Lauren. She told me she had felt shy at first, too.

The lights went out, and Josh's mum brought in a huge cake with candles.

We all sang *Happy Birthday*. Josh blew out the candles and made a wish.

After tea we
played hide
and seek ...

pin the tail on
the donkey ...

24

a balloon game ...

and musical chairs.

I didn't win a
prize, but I had
a brilliant time.

25

Then Dad came back.
It was time to go already!

27

Today I got two letters!
One was from Josh, saying
thank you for the present.

The other was from Lauren,
inviting me to
another party.
I can't wait!

# Notes for parents and teachers

This book introduces children to the experience of going to a party. Parents and teachers may find it useful to stop and discuss issues as they come up in the book.

Parties are fun, but they often introduce new settings and unfamiliar situations. New challenges may include practical matters such as finding the way around an unfamiliar house or venue, encountering new foods, and taking in a lot of new information such as the rules of games. Making a costume for a fancy dress party can be a challenge both for children and parents.

Emotional challenges may include meeting a number of people at once and learning to be part of a group. Some children find it hard to share adult attention and not to be the focus of attention. Others find it difficult to be a good loser.

Some children feel shy on entering a party, and may even experience an attack of 'pre-party nerves' before the occasion. They may be worried by the idea of being offered food they don't like. They may, like this book's main character, feel resentful at the prospect of giving rather than receiving. Encourage the children to talk about their feelings. Fears and worries can often be allayed by stressing the many positive aspects of parties.

Reread the story together, encouraging the children to take on the roles of different characters. Have they ever felt shy or jealous, like the characters in the story?

If children have already been to parties, encourage them to talk about their own experiences, using the book as a framework. They could make up stories about their ideal party, or a party that turned into their worst nightmare. They could make a list of their favourite party games, design an invitation, or design a costume for a fancy dress party. A party may introduce new words, including: invitation, fancy dress, costume, present, prize. Explain what these words mean.

## Use this book for teaching literacy

This book can help you in the literacy hour in the following ways:

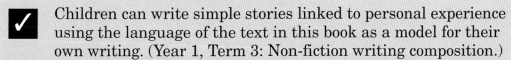 Children can write simple stories linked to personal experience using the language of the text in this book as a model for their own writing. (Year 1, Term 3: Non-fiction writing composition.)

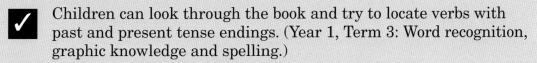 Children can look through the book and try to locate verbs with past and present tense endings. (Year 1, Term 3: Word recognition, graphic knowledge and spelling.)

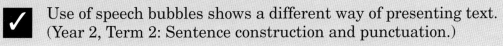 Use of speech bubbles shows a different way of presenting text. (Year 2, Term 2: Sentence construction and punctuation.)

# Books to read

*Jake's Birthday* by Rob Lewis (Red Fox, 1994)
Jake the badger's birthday is coming soon, but his brother Henry
has a birthday first. As Henry's birthday dawns, Jake finds it hard
to join in the fun. He wants his own cake and presents now, not in
two weeks' time.

*The Birthday Party* by Althea (A & C Black, 1996)
Lee hates parties, so he is dismayed when his best friend Andy gives
him a party invitation. At Andy's house, Lee feels so shy he almost
runs away. But the party turns out to be
more fun than he expects.

*Going to a Party* by Anne Civardi
and Stephen Cartright
(Usborne Publishing, 1992)
Nellie and Ned are invited to a
fancy dress party. Their monster
costumes are a big hit at the party,
and everyone wins a prize.